SECOND EDITION

PRO-ROLLER™

PILATES ESSENTIALS

Angela Kneale, OTR
Occupational Therapist
Certified Pilates Instructor

PRO-ROLLER™ Pilates Essentials, Second Edition

Published by:
OPTP
Tools for fitness. Knowledge for health.
3800 Annapolis Lane, Suite 165
Minneapolis, Minnesota 55447
800.367.7393
www.optp.com

Printed in the United States of America

Cover and Interior Design: Steve Bubb
Photography: TJ Thoraldson Photography
Photography Producer: Dani Hartmann
PRO-ROLLER™ Model: Christy Lyons
Technical Editors: Georgia L. Norgren, DPT, Susanne Schaars, MSPT, Dip.MDT

ISBN: 978-0-9843724-2-3

Every effort has been made to ensure that the information contained in this publication is accurate and current at the time of printing. The ideas, exercises, and suggestions are not intended as a substitute for consulting with your healthcare provider. All matters regarding your health require medical supervision. Neither the author nor the publisher shall be liable or responsible for any loss, injury, or damage allegedly arising from any information or suggestion in this publication.

Consult your physician or healthcare professional before starting any type of exercise program, especially if you have health concerns.

Contents

Getting Rolling 1
Aligning 4
Finding Center 6
Breathing 8
Imprint and Release 9
Spine Rolls 10
Ribcage Arms 11
Knee Lift 12
Bend and Stretch 13
Shoulder Reach.................................... 14
Shoulder Blade Squeeze..................... 15
Arm Scissors 16
V to W.. 17
Arm Circles.. 18
Arm Wrap 19
Abdominal Curl.................................... 20
Dying Bug.. 21
Breast Stroke....................................... 22
Shell Stretch 23
Hundred 24
Mid-Back Extension 25
Half Roll Back 26
Obliques Roll Back.............................. 27
Spine Twist 28
Cat Stretch 29
Leg Extension...................................... 30
Knee Stretch 31
Saw.. 32
Triceps Press 33
Bridge 34
Hip Release 35
Toe Taps 36
Bookends 37
Leg Scissors.. 38
Bicycle... 39
Frog Legs 40
Hip Sway 41
One Leg Kick....................................... 42
Sternum Drop...................................... 43
Spine Stretch Forward 44
Swan 45
Mermaid 46
Diagonal Mermaid 47
Lunge Series 48
PRO-ROLLER™ Pilates Essentials 50
Today, I will... 52
Acknowledgements............................. 52
References 52

"Physical fitness is the first requisite to happiness."

Joseph Pilates

Getting Rolling

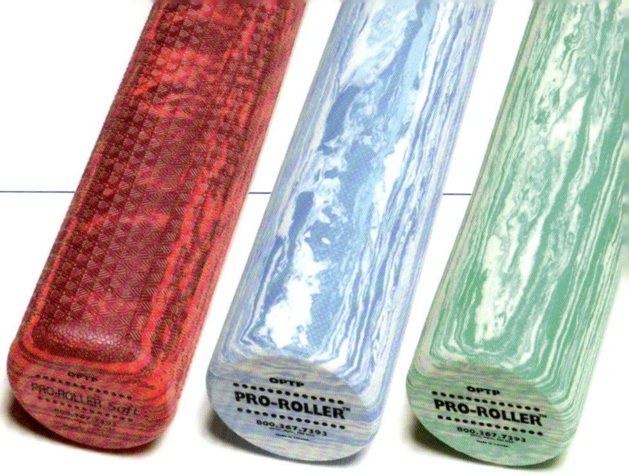

Pilates has been called the ultimate mind-body exercise, a whole approach to movement based on the work of Joseph Pilates (1880-1967). Incorporating the PRO-ROLLER™ with Pilates exercise creates additional awareness of how your body feels and moves, helping develop better posture and body symmetry, while challenging core strength and balance. The PRO-ROLLER™ is an excellent teaching tool, providing opportunities to playfully experience movement that targets strength and flexibility, and decreases muscle stress and tension.

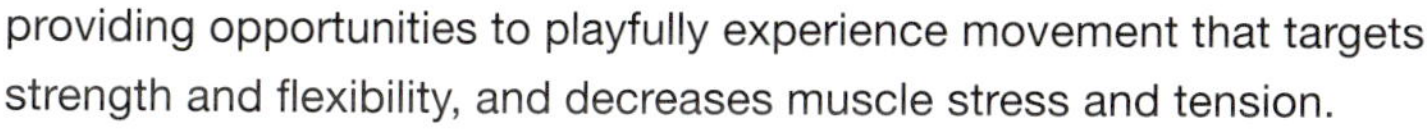

Cylindrical-shaped foam rollers once served only as packing material, and now have been adopted by physical therapists, movement educators, and fitness instructors throughout the world. Dr. Moshe Feldenkrais (1902-1984), physicist and founder of the Feldenkrais Method, was one of the first people to begin using foam rollers as a therapeutic device. Rehabilitation professionals utilize foam rollers for muscle reeducation, dynamic strengthening, enhancing balance reactions, increasing flexibility of muscles and nerves, and challenging sensory and movement systems.

Over time, foam roller manufacturing has improved to offer high quality, long-lasting rollers that maintain their shape, even with heavy use. With closed-cell structure and cross-linked foam technology, the PRO-ROLLER™ series of rollers is both comfortable and durable. Keep your PRO-ROLLER™ accessible, so you know you'll use it often. When not in use, it should be stored lying flat—avoid stacking anything heavy on top that could cause dents. Use mild soap and water to clean.

The green marble and blue marble rollers are made of the same moderately firm, yet comfortable density and are ideal for Pilates movements. The pink marble PRO-ROLLER™ Soft is softer in density and provides more gentle support. PRO-ROLLER™ Pilates exercises are ideally performed on a firm, flat surface such as the floor, an exercise mat, or a low exercise table. Choose comfortable clothing in which you can move freely. Leave feet bare or wear socks with a grip surface.

This publication provides many of the basics you would find in a beginning Pilates class, but is not meant to substitute for individual or group sessions with a qualified instructor.

Always listen to your body, and choose only the movements that feel comfortable.

As you get started, keep these guidelines in mind:

- Listen to your body and its own capabilities; choose only the movements that feel comfortable. Never force any movement or try to go beyond your limit.
- Stop and rest if, during any exercise, you experience discomfort or feel light-headed.
- Progress gradually. Start with simple movements, and build on your successes.
- Perform exercises slowly for maximum strengthening benefits.
- Allow your natural breath pattern to set the pace, avoiding excess tension.

The PRO-ROLLER™ invites you to spend time doing Pilates exercises that feel good to your body—above all, choose movements that are fun and enjoyable.

Joseph Pilates described his method as a way to connect and develop the mind, body, and spirit for lifelong health. His writings identified several concepts that underlie the meaning and effectiveness of his whole body exercise system. Learning Pilates is an evolving process, continually gaining insights and exploring mindfulness during movement.

Key Pilates principles include:

Alignment
Attending to proper alignment and the design of your body allows safe, effective use of muscles in balanced ways.

Control
Engaging the mind for conscious control means understanding and experiencing the form, function, alignment, and amount of effort during an exercise.

Fluidity
Dynamic, graceful movement flows as movement patterns are integrated into a smooth, rhythmic whole body experience.

Centering
Movement begins in the mind, then initiates and radiates outward from your body's center. Pilates emphasizes a strong and resilient center, supporting dynamic movements.

Concentration
Pilates exercise addresses both mental and physical training, requiring continual awareness of how your body is moving. Your focused attention keeps you in the present moment, deepening your understanding and increasing the benefits of the movement.

Precision
Movement precision honors the body's design while emphasizing appropriate effort and efficient use of your muscles, encouraging whole body integration.

Breath
Awareness of breathing links the body and mind. Breathing is harmonized with each movement to focus attention, improve the flow of oxygen, calm the body and mind, and activate targeted muscles.

PRO-ROLLER™ Pilates exercises utilize the roller in a variety of positions—sitting, standing, lying on one's back, front, or side, kneeling, as well as on hands and knees.

To lie on your back on the PRO-ROLLER™, first sit on the bottom edge of the roller with your hands on the floor on either side. Slowly lower your spine down onto the roller, using arms to help control your movement. Be certain that your head and your spine are fully supported on the roller.

If you are too tall to support your sacrum at one end of the roller and your head at the other, try putting the ends of two rollers together.

When getting off the roller, gently roll to your side, easing onto the floor.

Changing and improving your mind-body relationship requires perception inward into your body—pausing and paying attention. Spending time simply lying on the roller provides an ideal opportunity for noticing and experiencing your brain-body systems. Begin by observing your breathing for a minute or two... Then observe any areas of your body that feel tight or tense, and other areas that may benefit from increased activation. Common areas of tension include the lower back, neck, shoulders, and middle back between the shoulder blades. And it's true that many people could benefit from more tone in the abdomen and hip regions.

With some playful exploration, tune in to how your body feels on the PRO-ROLLER™. This unstable, rolling surface awakens your body's senses—experiencing heightened awareness of the position of your bones, joints, and muscles while balancing on the roller, as well as during movements. You will start to communicate directly with your body—fully experiencing each movement and noticing how motion of one body part, even just lifting your arm, creates subtle changes throughout your entire body.

Sweep one arm out along the floor—to the side and up as though making a snow angel, and feel how your shoulder blade rotates and glides along the back of your ribcage. As your arm arcs sideways, observe the rotational movement of your collarbone in front of your shoulder, and feel the gliding, rolling motions of your upper arm bone at the shoulder joints. These rhythms of your bones counter-rotating occur naturally throughout your body to create balanced, efficient movement (Franklin, 1996).

Think for a moment about the shoulder muscles as your arm sweeps. Muscles are bundles of many fibers, and each skeletal muscle fiber is made up of filaments that slide together and apart, creating the movement of the bones. As your arm moves away from your body, filaments of the deltoid muscle at the outside of your shoulder slide past one another, concentrically contracting or shortening. As you slowly lower your arm to your side, the deltoid muscle lengthens as the filaments slide apart—the eccentric phase of muscle activity. During exercise, it is important to experience full movement of each muscle group—both the shortening and lengthening phases of muscle action.

While you have been lying on the PRO-ROLLER™, you most likely have discovered how the muscles at the center of your body actively keep you balanced and centered, preventing you from rolling off! Exploring this dynamic stabilization is well suited to Pilates exercise, with the roller helping to act as your body's instructor—communicating with your body's senses, ensuring your focus and concentration, and fully experiencing the movement of your muscles, bones, and joints.

Aligning

Alignment is a whole-body sensation, created by balanced interaction of joints, muscles, and body systems for efficient and healthy movement (Franklin, 2009). Alignment is not a fixed posture based on holding a certain position, but is flexible and free and moves without effort (Franklin, 2006). Although there is no "perfect" posture, an "ideal" posture keeps the stresses on the body evenly distributed so that joints are bearing weight comfortably and muscles are working optimally. Ideal posture is not rigid and tense, but instead is lengthened and aligned, and ready for movement.

Discovering your body's central axis helps to balance and align your body's posture with ease. Try visualizing one plane that divides your body into equal right and left halves, and another plane that divides your body into equal front and back halves. The intersection of these two planes creates a line—a central axis around which your body is functionally organized.

The goal of exercise and postural training is functional, proficient, and healthful movement. If you exercise with tension and poor posture, you will actually feel tenser afterward and will have reinforced your poor posture. Instead, train with concentration and positive imagery, encouraging good posture and balanced muscle tone—becoming what you practice (Franklin, 2009).

Centered, balanced alignment feels good to your body, and provides the basis for freedom of movement in all directions. Each body position is a momentary event within a flow of movement, creating dynamic alignment (Franklin, 2006).

Awareness of your body and how it functions is important during Pilates exercise. Most often you will start and end each movement with centered, balanced spine alignment. An ideally aligned spine runs down the center of your body as viewed from the front or back, and from the side it displays an "S" of balanced natural curves.

Aligned spine
balanced natural curves

When lying on your back on the PRO-ROLLER™, ensure that your head and your spine are fully supported, and knees are bent, with your feet flat on the floor at hip-distance apart. Slowly rock from side to side, comparing the feeling of rocking right and left, and then center your spine lengthwise on the roller.

Gently tilt your pelvis forward and backward, noticing how the motion affects all the curves of your spine, and then find the midpoint position between—balancing the curves. Typically, the top front points (anterior superior iliac spines) of your pelvis will be level with the pubic bone.

With your spine aligned, you will be able to feel the natural spaces of the gentle "C" curves behind your neck and lower back, as well as the backward "C" curve at the upper middle back supported on the roller.

Joseph Pilates' theories promote awareness and appreciation of the body and how it moves, and can be applied to any exercise or activity for integrative, efficient, and healthy movement.

The PRO-ROLLER™ is an effective training tool during Pilates exercise, providing sensory feedback that directly teaches your body and mind, encouraging symmetry between both sides of your body, as well as balanced muscle tone—relaxing your tense muscles and activating less-toned muscles. PRO-ROLLER™ Pilates exercises help you to playfully explore how your bones, joints, and muscles continually support your body's dynamic alignment.

Finding Center

Our bodies are designed for movement—every day in all directions. Each movement initiates from your body's center, the core muscles that support your spine during daily activities as well as exercise. The Pilates method targets a resilient, strong center that provides core stability, with a spine that moves freely, and with control in all planes of motion. The body's core is three-dimensional, with muscles spanning from the ribcage to the pelvis, the low back, and hips. Connecting with your core muscles will maximize your benefits from Pilates exercise.

Core muscles include deep muscles such as transversus abdominis, lumbar multifidus, pelvic floor, and diaphragm, as well as outer layers of muscles—obliques, rectus abdominis, iliopsoas, quadratus lumborum, erector spinae, and gluteals. Your inner core muscles function together, supporting your body's systems. Your inner core works in concert with your outer core to provide dynamic stability and coordinated mobility—bending your spine forward and backward, rotating, and side bending.

The key to finding your center during Pilates is thinking about and feeling the muscles of your inner core. Try visualizing your inner core as a supportive cylinder, with transversus abdominis enclosing the front and sides of the cyliinder, multifidus in back, diaphragm at the top of the cylinder, and pelvic floor muscles at the bottom.

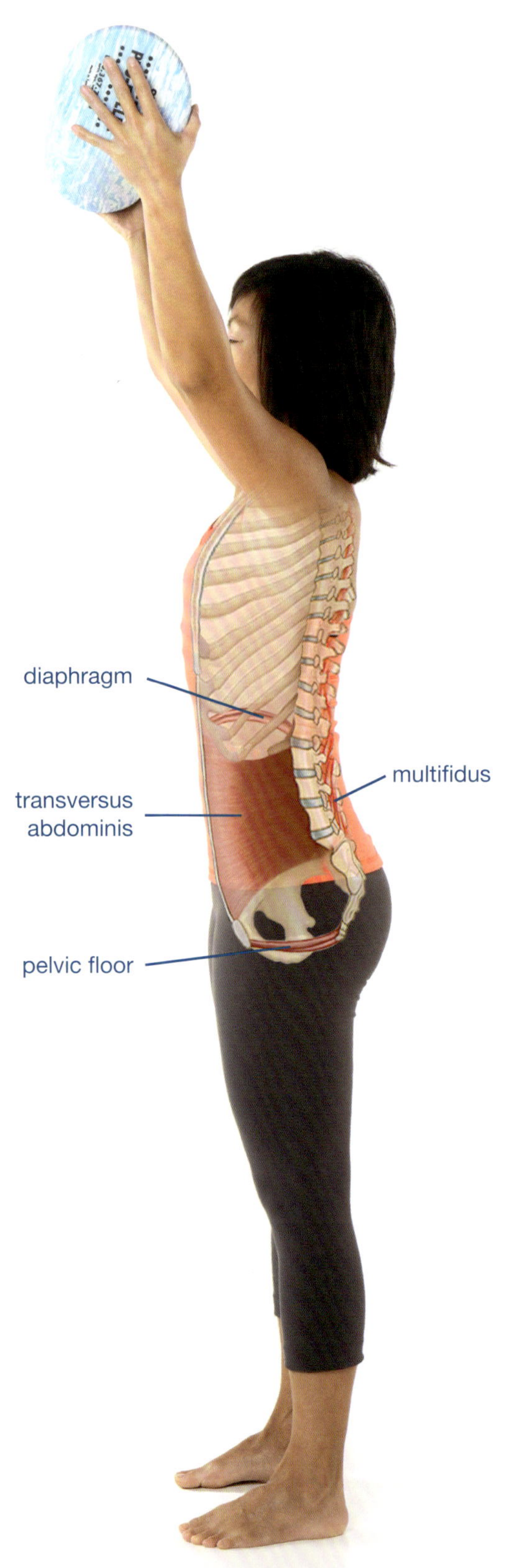

With every breath, inner core muscles work together to support your body's center. Focusing attention on these subtle motions helps improve the overall efficiency and function of your body's core, and integrate movements into a whole body experience.

Pilates exercises encourage both concentric and eccentric contraction of transversus abdominis, gently bracing your lower abdomen. These muscle fibers wrap horizontally from front to back like a corset, and they can best be felt at the bikini line. Feel how the front of your pelvis slightly narrows as you breathe in, and widens as the abdomen flattens while breathing out. Also notice that when laughing or coughing, transversus abdominis tightens to protect your internal organs.

Multifidus, which connects the vertebral segments of your low back, works together with transversus abdominis to support your inner core and promote a healthy back.

When you breathe deeply and exhale fully, the dome-shaped diaphragm lowers and lifts in your abdomen, facilitating the expansion and contraction of your deep inner core muscles.

Think of the pelvic floor as a diamond-shaped muscular trampoline (supportive, taut, flexible) at the bottom of the pelvic opening, from the pubic bone in front, the left and right sit bones, and the tailbone in back. During inhalation, these four points move slightly away from one another as the pelvic floor muscles lengthen and widen. During exhalation, imagine bringing the four points closer together without clenching, then gently lifting that center point up like an elevator in the lower abdomen.

Inhale, feeling the expansion of your lungs, ribcage, and abdomen, the widening of sit bones and pelvic floor, and the narrowing at the top front of your pelvis. As you exhale, the pelvic floor lifts, as if walking into cold water, and the front of the pelvis widens, flattening the abdomen. Additional layers of abdominal muscles then activate by gently tightening to draw your abdomen toward your spine—as if you were zipping up a tight pair of jeans from your pubic bone to your belly button.

PRO-ROLLER™ Pilates exercises promote a resilient core, activating inner core muscles that provide support, as well as outer layers of muscles, effectively strengthening your body from the inside out.

Breathing

Breathing is an integral principle of Pilates, harmonized with each movement as you engage core muscles and release unnecessary tension, allowing you to focus on each moment. If you were to include only one Pilates principle within your daily life, awareness of your breathing would have the greatest impact. Often our breathing patterns have become shallow, utilizing less than half of our lung capacities, and relying on secondary chest muscles. Instead, optimal breathing is diaphragmatic—this full, natural breathing pattern effectively oxygenates your body and calms your neuromuscular system.

Begin each Pilates exercise session with focused breathing and gentle movements to reconnect your body and mind.

Starting Position

Lie on the roller, with your head supported and spine aligned. Knees bent, feet hip-width apart.

Inhale

Feel your breath expanding three-dimensionally into the back, sides, and front of your ribcage and abdomen. Notice the widening of your sit bones and lengthening of pelvic floor muscles, and the support of transversus abdominis at the front of your pelvis.

Exhale

Gently activate pelvic floor and abdominal muscles, and experience the flattening of the abdomen and widening at the front of the pelvis. Feel the ribs releasing in toward the center of your body and sliding slightly downward toward your pelvis.

- Allow your natural breathing pace—rhythmic, slow, relaxed, and flowing.
- Notice the three-dimensional expansion during inhalation as the diaphragm lowers in the abdomen.
- As you exhale, experience abdominal engagement, flattening your abdomen as the diaphragm lifts.
- Exhale completely, encouraging your next breath to be full and natural.

Imprint and Release

Benefits

Trains sequence of core activation.

Starting Position

Lie on the roller, aligned spine. Knees bent, with feet hip-width apart.

Movement Sequence

To prepare—inhale; breath expands, pelvic floor muscles lengthen and widen.

Exhale

Activate pelvic floor and abdominals, and gently flatten your low back toward the roller while keeping gluteal muscles relaxed, feeling your ribcage and pelvis coming closer together by about an inch.

Inhale

Slowly return your pelvis and spine to starting position.

Repeat 5–8 times.

natural curve

imprint

- Utilize the imprint position to support your low back during any exercise with both legs in the air.
- Feel pelvic floor muscle filaments sliding together during imprint, and apart as you release.
- Feel outer layer abdominal muscle filaments sliding together during imprint, and then apart.
- Notice the sequence of pelvic floor and abdominal muscle activation, keeping gluteals relaxed.

Spine Rolls

Benefits

Promotes segmental spinal mobility; strengthens core and hips.

Starting Position

Lie on the roller, aligned spine. Knees bent, feet hip-width apart.

Movement Sequence

To prepare—inhale; breath expands, pelvic floor widens.

Exhale

Imprint your low back using abdominals, then activate gluteals to tilt your pelvis back; and sequentially peel your spine off the roller, vertebra by vertebra, to your upper middle back, while your neck stays relaxed.

Inhale

Maintain your body in a bridge position, and breathe three-dimensionally.

Exhale

With core support, sequentially roll each vertebra of your spine back down onto the roller.

Inhale

Release to starting position.

Repeat 5–8 times.

- Articulate through each segment as you evenly roll your spine off and on the roller.
- Place each vertebra down individually, at a distance from the vertebrae already on the roller.
- Imprint spine (page 9) first using abdominals, then use gluteals and hamstrings to tilt and lift pelvis.

Ribcage Arms

Benefits

Challenges balance and core stability.

Starting Position

Lie on the roller, aligned spine. Knees bent, feet hip-width apart, arms long at your sides.

Movement Sequence

Inhale

Lift your arms toward the ceiling.

Exhale

Activate your core muscles, feeling the connection of your ribcage to your pelvis, as reach your arms overhead.

Inhale

Lift arms toward the ceiling.

Exhale

Activate core muscles as arms return to stating position.

Repeat 5–8 times.

- Experience the dynamic stability of your core, staying centered on the roller during arm movement.
- Sense your ribcage sliding toward your pelvis, feeling core support as your arms reach overhead.
- Feel your shoulder blades rotating and gliding along your ribcage as your arms reach.

Knee Lift

Benefits

Integrates core and lower body movements.

Starting Position

Lie on the roller, aligned spine. Knees bent, feet hip-width apart.

Movement Sequence

Inhale

Breath expands three-dimensionally.

Exhale

Activate your core, and flex at your hip to lift your knee toward your chest.

Inhale

Maintain relaxed, lifted knee position.

Exhale

Activate core, and slowly lower your leg down to starting position.

Repeat 5–8 times, alternating sides.

- Experience the dynamic stability of your core as you lift each leg, staying centered on the roller.
- Deepen the crease of your hip as you lift your knee, sinking the femur into your hip joint.
- Feel your torso resting into the roller, and your shoulders, neck, and jaw relaxed.
- Gently press your big toe and second toe into the floor, if needed to assist with stability.

Bend and Stretch

Benefits

Stretches and strengthens leg muscles; mobilizes ankle, knee, and hip joints.

Starting Position

Lie on the roller, aligned spine. Knees bent, feet hip-width apart.

Movement Sequence

Inhale

Lift your leg, with knee bent and ankle flexed, folding at your hip joint.

Exhale

Activate your core, and slowly stretch your leg out to full length, softly pointing your toes.

Inhale

Slowly bend your ankle, knee, and hip, again folding at your hip joint.

Exhale

Activate core, and return your leg back to the starting position.

Repeat 8–10 times, alternating sides.

- Experience the dynamic stability of your core as your leg moves, staying centered on the roller.
- Deepen the crease of your hip as you bend your leg, sinking the femur into your hip joint.
- During leg movement, knee aligns with center of foot, as upper and lower leg bones counter-rotate.
- Variations: Leg turned out from your hip, or turned in from your hip.

Shoulder Reach

Benefits

Improves shoulder mobility; integrates core and upper body.

Starting Position

Lie on the roller, aligned spine. Knees bent, feet hip-width apart, arms long and lifted toward ceiling, with palms facing one another.

Movement Sequence

Inhale

Reach fingertips to the ceiling, shoulder blades move away from one another.

Exhale

With strong core, keep elbows straight, and slide shoulder blades back and down.

Repeat 5–8 times.

- Experience the dynamic stability of your core during arm movements, staying centered on the roller.
- Allow the shoulder blades to glide freely around the ribcage as arms reach to the ceiling.
- Feel your shoulder blades relax back down, flat against the ribcage, gently hugging the roller.

Shoulder Blade Squeeze

Benefits

Improves shoulder mobility; integrates core and upper body.

Starting Position

Lie on the roller, aligned spine. Knees bent, feet hip-width apart, arms out to the sides at shoulder-level, elbows bent, and palms facing toward feet.

Movement Sequence

To prepare—inhale; breath expands three-dimensionally.

Exhale

Activate core, and gently squeeze shoulder blades back together around the roller, lowering your elbows down toward the floor.

Inhale

Slowly release your shoulder blades back to starting position.

Repeat 5–8 times.

- Experience the dynamic stability of your core during arm movements, staying centered on the roller.
- Allow your shoulder blades to glide freely along the ribcage, gently hugging the roller.
- If experiencing shoulder problems, start with your arms closer to the sides of your body.

Arm Scissors

Benefits

Improves shoulder mobility; integrates core and upper body.

Starting Position

Lie on the roller, aligned spine. Knees bent, feet hip-width apart, arms long and lifted toward ceiling, with palms facing one another.

Movement Sequence

Inhale

Breath expands three-dimensionally.

Exhale

Activate core, and reach one arm overhead and the other arm down alongside your pelvis.

Inhale

Lift arms again toward ceiling.

Exhale

With strong core, reach opposite arm overhead and the other arm down by your pelvis.

Repeat 8–10 times.

- Experience the dynamic stability of your core during arm movements, staying centered on the roller.
- Move smoothly and evenly with both arms, allowing shoulder blades to glide along the ribcage.
- Feel the weight of your collarbones on the sternum, releasing upper body tension as arms move.

V to W

Benefits

Improves shoulder mobility; releases upper body tension.

Starting Position

Lie on the roller, aligned spine. Knees bent, feet hip-width apart.

Movement Sequence

Inhale

Reach arms overhead in V position, with palms up.

Exhale

Activate core, and pull elbows toward your sides to create W-shape with arms.

Repeat 5–8 times.

- Feel the open, spaciousness across the front of your chest and shoulders, releasing upper body tension.
- Notice the rotational gliding of your shoulder blades as arms reach out and pull down.
- Experience the dynamic stability of your core during arm movements, staying centered on the roller.
- If comfortable, touch the floor with the back of your hands for additional stretch across chest.

Arm Circles

Benefits
Increased shoulder mobility; integrates core and upper body.

Starting Position
Lie on the roller, aligned spine. Knees bent, feet hip-width apart, arms long at your sides.

Movement Sequence

Inhale
Maintain abdominal connection as you lift arms overhead, keeping ribcage in contact with roller.

Exhale
With activated core, circle your arms out to the sides and around toward your hips.

Repeat 5 times each direction.

- Experience the dynamic stability of your core during arm movements, staying centered on the roller.
- Both arms move smoothly and evenly, with shoulder blades gliding along the ribcage.
- Feel the weight of your collarbones on the sternum, releasing upper body tension as arms move.

Arm Wrap

Benefits

Improves shoulder mobility; releases upper body tension.

Start

Lie on the roller, aligned spine. Knees bent, feet hip-width apart, arms out to sides.

Movement Sequence

To prepare—inhale; breath expands three-dimensionally.

Exhale

Activate core, and wrap arms across chest as though giving yourself a hug.

Inhale

Open your arms out to sides.

Repeat 5–8 times.

- Wrap right arm over left, open arms, and then left arm over right, alternating with each exhale.
- Experience the dynamic stability of your core during arm movements, staying centered on the roller.
- Allow shoulder blades to glide around your ribcage, releasing upper body tension.

Abdominal Curl

Benefits

Activates your core; trains sequence of upper body flexion.

Starting Position

Lie on the roller, aligned spine. Knees bent, feet hip-width apart, hands behind head with elbows reaching out.

Movement Sequence

Inhale

Gently nod your head forward to lengthen through the back of your neck, prior to lifting your head off the roller.

Exhale

Activate abdominals and curl your upper body off the roller to your middle back, sliding the ribcage closer to the pelvis while keeping your pelvis level.

Inhale

Maintain curved upper body, abdominals flattened.

Exhale

With abdominal support, slowly lower your upper body back down to the roller.

Repeat 5–8 times.

- Emphasize inner core strength to keep your pelvis stable and centered; avoid curling upper body too high.
- Allow gliding of your ribcage toward your pelvis, gliding of shoulder blades, avoiding upper body tension.
- Feel outer abdominal muscle filaments sliding together as you curl forward, and then sliding apart.
- Core challenge: From curled position, roll only halfway back, and then curve forward again.

Dying Bug

Benefits

Integrates core, upper, and lower body movement; challenges core stability.

Starting Position

Lie on the roller, aligned spine, knees bent, feet hip-width apart. Lift one knee toward your chest and opposite arm toward the ceiling.

Movement Sequence

To prepare—inhale; breath expands three-dimensionally.

Exhale

Activate core, reach your arm overhead while lengthening your leg parallel to the floor.

Inhale

Slowly return your arm and leg to starting position.

Repeat 8–10 times on each side.

- Reach your arm and opposite leg away from your strong core, staying centered on roller.
- Allow gliding of your shoulder blade as your arm moves freely and smoothly.
- Deepen the crease of your hip as you bend your leg, sinking the femur into your hip joint.
- To assist stability, gently press the big toe and second toe of your supporting leg into the floor.

Breast Stroke

Benefits

Strengthens muscles of middle back; improves posture.

Starting Position

Lie on the floor on your front with aligned spine, with legs together or slightly apart, pelvis resting into the floor. Arms long overhead, with forearms wide apart on roller.

Movement Sequence

Inhale

Slide your shoulder blades down your back.

Exhale

Activate core muscles, lengthen and extend your upper torso while keeping your bottom rib in contact with the floor. Open your elbows wide, and roll the roller beneath your forehead.

Inhale

Maintain lifted position, reaching your sternum away from your toes.

Exhale

Lengthen your upper body back down, slowly controlling return to starting position.

Repeat 5–8 times.

- Feel upper and middle back extensor muscle filaments sliding together as you lift, then apart.
- Keep your head in line with your spine, with eyes looking at the roller during spine extension.
- Feel your shoulder blades gliding back and down while your upper body lifts.
- Experience core support, keeping your bottom rib and lower body resting into the floor.

Shell Stretch

Benefits
Releases low back and shoulder tension.

Starting Position
Sit back on your heels, knees bent at hip-width apart, arms on roller.

Movement Sequence

Inhale
Curve your spine, rolling the roller toward you.

Exhale
Engage abdominals, and roll the roller away from you, lengthening your lower back and releasing your shoulders and arms.

Repeat 5–8 times.

- Sink your tailbone toward the floor, lengthening your lower back as the roller rolls away.
- As you exhale, release any excess tension in your lower back, shoulders, and arms.
- If experiencing knee discomfort, try a folded blanket or pillow beneath your seat.

Hundred

Benefits

Energizes body; improves circulation; promotes endurance.

Starting Position

Sit on the floor, with the roller crosswise behind you, knees bent, feet hip-width apart. Gently lean back into the roller at the bottom of your shoulder blades, low back imprinted, arms long by sides with palms down.

Movement Sequence

Inhale for 5 counts

Maintain imprinted spine, pulse from your shoulders with small vertical arm movements as if you are pressing on springs.

Exhale for 5 counts

Continue pulsing arms, and activate core to lift your pelvis off the floor.

Continue for 100 counts.

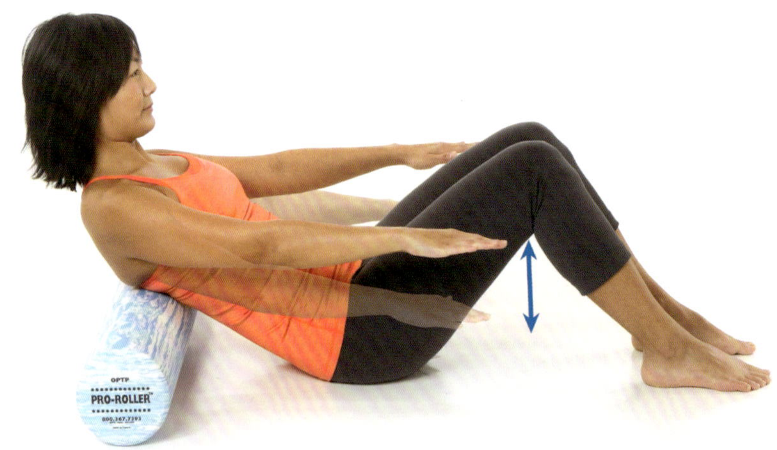

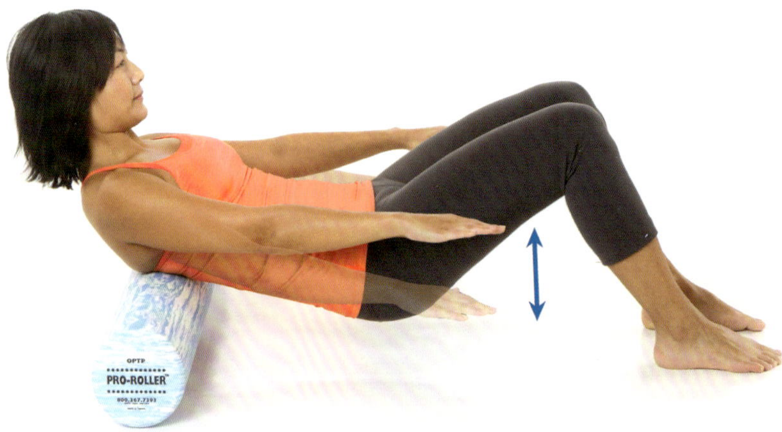

- Experience core connection, lifting your plevis as you exhale and lowering pelvis while you inhale.
- Stay wide across front and back of shoulders, with pumping movement from your shoulder joints.
- Allow the weight of your sternum to rest into your chest, avoiding upper body tension.
- If experiencing neck tension, place one hand behind your head for support.

Mid-Back Extension

Benefits

Integrates breathing with spinal movement; improves posture; lengthens the spine.

Starting Position

Sit on the floor with the roller crosswise behind you, knees bent, feet hip-width apart. Gently lean back into the roller at the bottom of your shoulder blades, elbows reaching wide, hands supporting the weight of your head.

Movement Sequence

Inhale

Gently arch back over the roller, exploring the supported extension of your middle back.

Exhale

Activate core, slowly return to starting position.

Repeat 5–8 times.

- Breathing sets the rhythm of your movements; inhale into spinal extension, exhale easing forward.
- Extend your middle spine as far as feels comfortable, supported by your core muscles and the roller.
- Feel the open, spaciousness across your collarbones and the front your shoulders.

Half Roll Back

Benefits

Strengthens core; mobilizes pelvis and spine.

Starting Position

Sit tall and aligned, with your feet resting on the roller in front of you, hip-width apart. Knees bent, with arms long and parallel to floor, palms facing one another.

Movement Sequence

Inhale

Breath expands three-dimensionally.

Exhale

Engage abdominals to roll your pelvis away from your legs, curving your spine into a "C" shape as you roll back.

Inhale

Maintain curved spine position.

Exhale

Engage abdominals to roll forward again to vertical pelvis, sitting tall.

Repeat 5–8 times.

- Begin by rolling your pelvis away from your legs, opening the front of your hips.
- Feel abdominal muscle filaments sliding together during spine flexion, apart as spine lengthens.
- Allow shoulder blades to glide along your ribcage, keeping neck and jaw relaxed.
- Core challenge: Reach the roller away from you, lengthening your legs as you roll down.

Obliques Roll Back

Benefits

Strengthens core; mobilizes pelvis and spine.

Starting Position

Sit tall and aligned, with your feet resting on the roller in front of you, hip-width apart. Knees bent, with arms long and parallel to floor, palms facing one another.

Movement Sequence

To prepare—inhale; breath expands three-dimensionally.

Exhale

Engage abdominals to roll your pelvis away from your legs, curving your spine into a "C" shape as you roll back, simultaneously rotating upper body and sweeping one arm out to side, turning palm up.

Inhale

Maintain abdominal connection to return to center and roll forward to vertical pelvis, sweeping arm forward again.

Repeat 5 times, alternating sides.

- Begin by rolling your pelvis away from your legs, opening the front of your hips, as your spine rotates.
- Feel oblique abdominal muscle filaments sliding together and apart during spinal rotation and return to center.
- Return your pelvis back to vertical, with body weight evenly on your sit bones.
- Core challenge: Reach the roller away from you, lengthening your legs as you roll down.

Spine Twist

Benefits

Promotes segmental spinal motion; enhances flexibility.

Start

Sit tall, aligned spine, with legs long and together. Hold the roller just below shoulder height, gently pressing hands into ends of roller.

Movement Sequence

To prepare—inhale; breath expands three-dimensionally.

Exhale

Activate core, and slowly rotate your torso for 3 counts, bending the back elbow

Inhale

Return to center, spiraling up from lower spine, lengthening through your central axis.

Repeat 5 times, alternating sides.

- Keep your nose and sternum in line with center of roller, allowing gliding of ribcage and shoulder blades.
- Rotate your torso around your central axis, like a merry-go-round, as your pelvis counter-rotates.
- Lengthen tall through your spine, visualizing central axis as you return to the center starting position.
- Alternate starting positions: Sit on a cushion, or with legs crossed.

Cat Stretch

Benefits

Activates core; promotes segmental spinal motion; enhances flexibility.

Starting Position

On hands and knees, aligned spine, with hands on roller, and knees under hips at hip-width apart.

Movement Sequence

Inhale

Breath expands three-dimensionally.

Exhale

Activate your core, sequentially curving each segment of your spine into flexion from your tailbone to your head.

Inhale

Breath expands into your back and ribcage, relaxing your head, neck, and shoulders.

Exhale

Sequentially uncurl your spine into slight extension, from tailbone to head.

Repeat 5–8 times.

- Curve evenly through your spine, experiencing the movement of each vertebra of your spine.
- Notice your sit bones moving closer together and pelvic floor activating as your spine curves.
- Experience the widening of your sit bones and pelvic floor as you uncurl and extend your spine.
- Allow gliding motions of your shoulder blades, ribcage, and pelvis during spine movements.

Single Leg Extension

Benefits

Integrates core, upper, and lower body; strengthens core.

Starting Position

On your hands and knees, with upper shins on the roller. Arms under shoulders, knees under hips, and spine aligned.

Movement Sequence

To prepare—inhale; breath expands three-dimensionally.

Exhale

Activate core, keeping torso and pelvis relatively centered, and slowly reach one leg behind you.

Inhale

Maintain strong center, and return your leg to starting position.

Repeat 8–10 times, alternating sides.

- Keep your pelvis centered, extending your leg from your hip, reaching your leg out to full length.
- Experience the dynamic stability of your core during your right and left leg movements.
- Core challenge: Reach your opposite arm forward as you extend your leg back.

Knee Stretch

Benefits

Integrates core, upper, and lower body; strengthens core.

Starting Position

On your hands and knees, with upper shins on the roller. Arms under shoulders, spine aligned.

Movement Sequence

To prepare—inhale; breath expands three-dimensionally.

Exhale

Engage abdominals and flex your hips to pull the knees and the roller in toward your chest, curving your spine.

Inhale

Extend your hips to return to the starting position.

Repeat 8–10 times.

- Experience your strong core as you pull your knees toward your chest, and as you press the roller out.
- Keep your shoulders over your wrists, and shoulder blades wide throughout the movement.
- Allow your head and neck to follow the line of the rest of your spine, curving as you pull in the knees.

Saw

Benefits

Improves spinal mobility; strengthens core.

Starting Position

Sit on the roller with weight evenly on sit bones, aligned spine. Legs straight and shoulder-width apart, ankles flexed.

Movement Sequence

Inhale

Rotate your spine around central axis, reaching arms out away from you.

Exhale

Activate core and curve forward from the top of your spine, reaching your front arm toward your little toe, as back arm reaches away and rotates, turning palm up.

Inhale

Roll up through your spine from bottom to top, with both arms reaching away.

Exhale

Rotate spine to face forward again, back arm rotates to return to starting position.

Repeat 5–8 times, alternating sides.

- First rotate your spine around central axis; then flex forward, with arms reaching away from you.
- Notice how your pelvis naturally moves in opposition to your spine, anchoring your sit bones.
- Keep your head movement in line with the rest of your spine, neck and jaw relaxed.
- Alternate starting positions: Bend knees slightly, or sit with legs crossed.

Triceps Press

Benefits

Strengthens upper body;
integrates core and upper body.

Starting Position

Sit tall on the floor, aligned spine, legs straight and together. Place hands on the roller behind you, elbows bent, fingertips facing forward.

Movement Sequence

To prepare—inhale; breath expands three-dimensionally.

Exhale

Activate core, and straighten your elbows, lifting your pelvis off the floor.

Inhale

Slowly bend your elbows to lower your body to the starting position.

Repeat 8–10 times.

- Experience your strong core keeping your pelvis centered throughout the movements.
- Feel muscle filaments of your triceps sliding together as elbows straighten, and apart as elbows bend.
- Feel muscle filaments of your biceps sliding apart as elbows straighten, and together as elbows bend.
- Breathing sets the rhythm of your movements as you press up, and slowly lower your body down.

Bridge

Benefits
Integrates core and lower body movement; strengthens core and lower body.

Starting Position
Lie on your back on the floor, aligned spine. Knees bent, feet on roller at hip-width apart.

Movement Sequence

Inhale
Breath expands three-dimensionally.

Exhale
Activate core, and extend your hips to lift pelvis off the floor, creating bridge position from knees to shoulders.

Inhale
Maintain bridge position, breath expands.

Exhale
Activate core, folding at hips to slowly lower pelvis back to floor.

Repeat 5–8 times.

- Experience your strong center supporting your body; gluteals and hamstrings extend your hips.
- Maintain the balanced symmetry of your pelvis, avoiding shifting or rotating toward one side.
- Sense your shoulder blades resting into the floor, with shoulders, neck, and jaw relaxed.

Hip Release

Benefits

Integrates core and lower body; improves hip mobility.

Starting Position

Lie on your back on the floor, aligned spine. Knees bent, legs and feet together with toes on the roller.

Movement Sequence

Inhale

Rotate and release your hips, lowering both knees out to the sides.

Exhale

Activate core and lengthen your legs out, pressing the roller away.

Inhale

Rotate legs to parallel, kneecaps face the ceiling.

Exhale

Activate core, gently pressing feet into the roller as you flex hips and knees to return to starting position.

Repeat 5–8 times.

- Allow each leg to gently fall to the side, sensing relaxation and release of your hip muscles.
- Keep the roller under control throughout exercise, activating core and gently pressing feet into the roller.
- Sense your shoulder blades resting into the floor, with shoulders, arms, neck, and jaw relaxed.

Toe Taps

Benefits

Strengthens core; integrates core and lower body.

Starting Position

Lie on your back with the roller crosswise beneath your sacrum, imprinted spine, shoulders relaxed, with hands holding the ends of the roller. Hips bent, knees relaxed, with shins parallel to the floor.

Movement Sequence

To prepare—inhale; breath expands three-dimensionally.

Exhale

Activate core, keeping pelvis stable, and hinge from your hip to slowly lower your bent leg, as if tapping your foot toward the floor.

Inhale

Bring your knee toward your chest again, folding at the hip, controlling return of leg to starting position.

Repeat 10 times, alternating sides.

- Lower your bent leg as far as you can maintain your pelvis centered, without tipping or shifting.
- Experience the support of your inner core, and imprint (page 9), with sacrum sinking into the roller.
- Sense your knees staying relaxed during leg movement, shoulder blades resting into the floor.
- Core challenge: Lower both legs simultaneously, hinging from your hips while keeping pelvis stable.

Book Ends

Benefits

Strengthens core; integrates core and lower body.

Starting Position

Lie on your back with the roller crosswise beneath your sacrum, imprinted spine, shoulders relaxed, with hands holding the ends of the roller. Legs together, reaching to the ceiling, flexed at the hips.

Movement Sequence

To prepare—inhale; breath expands three-dimensionally.

Exhale

Activate core, and slowly lower your leg(s) out to the side.

Inhale

Return your leg(s) to starting position.

Repeat 5 times alternating, and 5 times simultaneously.

- Lower each leg as far as you can maintain your pelvis centered, without tipping or shifting.
- Experience the support of your inner core, and imprint (page 9) with sacrum sinking into the roller.
- Feel inner thigh muscle filaments sliding apart as leg reaches to side, together as leg returns to center.
- Sense your shoulder blades resting into the floor, with shoulders, arms, neck, and jaw relaxed.

Leg Scissors

Benefits

Integrates core and lower body; promotes hip mobility.

Starting Position

Lie on your back with the roller crosswise beneath your sacrum, imprinted pelvis, shoulders relaxed, with hands holding the ends of the roller. Legs together, reaching to the ceiling, flexed at the hips.

Movement Sequence

Inhale

Breath expands three-dimensionally.

Exhale

Activate core, and slowly extend one leg out away from you, lowering toward the floor, while flexing at the hip to bring the other leg toward you.

Inhale

Control return of both legs to starting position.

Exhale

With strong core, switch legs to reach opposite leg away, and other leg toward you.

Repeat 8–10 times.

- Reach your legs away from your strong center, imprinting (page 9), with sacrum sinking into the roller.
- Feel front hip muscle filaments sliding apart as leg reaches away, together as leg flexes toward you.
- Feel muscle filaments at back of your hip sliding together as leg reaches away, apart as leg flexes.
- Sense your shoulder blades resting into the floor, with shoulders, arms, neck, and jaw relaxed.

Bicycle

Benefits
Integrates core and lower body; coordinates lower body movement.

Starting Position
Lie on your back with the roller crosswise beneath your sacrum, imprinted pelvis, shoulders relaxed, with hands holding the ends of the roller. Legs together, reaching to the ceiling, flexed at the hips.

Movement Sequence
From the Leg Scissors exercise, pedal your legs with smooth fluid motions.

Inhale
Scissor your legs, extending one leg toward the floor, flex the other toward you.

Exhale
Bend the knee of extended leg, reaching toes toward the floor.

Inhale
Bring bent leg toward you and straighten the knee; simultaneously extend your other leg.

Exhale
Bend the knee of other leg, reaching toes toward floor.

Repeat 8–10 times, then reverse direction.

- Experience fluid lower body movements—reaching legs straight as you inhale, bicycling as you exhale.
- Reach your legs away from your strong center, imprinting (page 9), with sacrum sinking into the roller.
- Feel front hip muscle filaments sliding apart as leg reaches away, together as leg flexes toward you.
- Feel muscle filaments at back of your hip sliding together as leg reaches away, apart as leg flexes.

Frog Legs

Benefits

Integrates core and lower body; improves hip mobility.

Starting Position

Lie on your back with the roller crosswise beneath your sacrum, imprinted pelvis, shoulders relaxed, with hands holding the ends of the roller. Hips turned out, knees apart and bent, with heels pressing together.

Movement Sequence

To prepare—inhale; breath expands three-dimensionally.

Exhale

Activate core, extend both legs out away from you, pressing inner legs together as you straighten.

Inhale

Control return of legs to starting position.

Repeat 8–10 times.

- Reach legs out as low as you can maintain your pelvic stability, imprinting (page 9) your low back.
- Experience the dynamic stability of your core, and keep the back of your sacrum sinking into the roller.
- Sense your shoulder blades resting into the floor, with shoulders, arms, neck, and jaw relaxed.

Hip Sway

Benefits
Activates core muscles; mobilizes pelvis and lower spine.

Starting Position
Lie on your back with the roller crosswise beneath your sacrum, imprinted pelvis, shoulders relaxed, with hands holding the ends of the roller. Legs together, hips and knees bent.

Movement Sequence

Inhale
Rotate lower torso, allowing both knees to lower toward the roller.

Exhale
Activate core and rotate your lower torso back to starting position.

Repeat 5–8 times, alternating sides.

- Experience core connection, with oblique abdominals supporting your spine during lower torso rotation.
- Lower your bent legs toward the roller, as low as you can keep your shoulder blades resting into the floor.
- Stay wide across the front of your shoulders and collarbones, neck and jaw relaxed.

One Leg Kick

Benefits

Integrates core, upper, and lower body; strengthens core,

Starting Position

Aligned spine plank position with forearms on floor, palms facing, elbows under shoulders, with your thighs on the roller at hip-width.

Movement Sequence

To prepare—inhale; breath expands three-dimensionally.

Exhale

Activate core muscles, and slowly bend your knee twice—once with toes pointed, once with ankle flexed.

Inhale

Lengthen your leg back to starting position.

Repeat 5–8 times, alternating legs.

- Experience your strong center, keeping torso and pelvis centered, without shifting or tilting.
- Feel quadriceps muscle filaments sliding apart as your knee bends, together as leg straightens.
- Feel hamstring muscle filaments sliding together as your knee bends, apart as leg straightens.

Sternum Drop

Benefits

Improves shoulder mobility and strength; integrates core and upper body.

Starting Position

Aligned spine plank position with forearms on floor, elbows under shoulders, with your thighs on the roller just above your knees.

Movement Sequence

Inhale

Slowly lower your sternum toward the floor, allowing your shoulder blades to move toward one another.

Exhale

With strong core, press your torso back to starting position, lifting your sternum and sliding your shoulder blades apart.

Repeat 8–10 times.

- Feel the support of your shoulder blade musculature, with slow controlled movements.
- Notice the smooth, gliding motions of your shoulder blades along your ribcage.
- Keep your head and neck in line with the rest of your spine, jaw relaxed.
- Experience your strong center, keeping torso and pelvis centered, without shifting or tilting.

Spine Stretch Forward

Benefits

Promotes segmental spinal motion during flexion; enhances flexibility.

Starting Position

Sit tall with aligned spine, legs crossed, with hands on roller in front of you.

Movement Sequence

Inhale

Lengthen through your spine.

Exhale

Engage abdominals, gently nod head forward, then slowly sequentially curving your spine forward, as if peeling away from a wall behind you, keeping pelvis vertical. Arms roll the roller forward.

Inhale

Maintain curved position of your spine, and breathe three-dimensionally.

Exhale

Roll your spine back up from bottom to top, returning to sitting tall with aligned spine.

Repeat 5–8 times.

- Slowly articulate through each segment of your spine while rolling down and rolling up.
- Press gently into the roller, experiencing your strong center supporting your body during movement.
- Alternate starting position: Sit with long legs, rolling the roller down on top of your legs as spine curves.

Swan

Benefits

Promotes segmental spinal mobility during extension; improves posture.

Starting Position

Lie on your front, aligned spine, legs extended and shoulder-width apart, with forearms on roller, palms down.

Movement Sequence

Inhale

Slide your shoulder blades down your back.

Exhale

With abdominal support, extend evenly through your spine from the top to the bottom as you roll the roller toward you.

Inhale

Maintain spinal extension, lifting sternum.

Exhale

Lengthen your spine back down to the floor, from bottom to top, reaching the top of your head away from your toes, rolling the roller away.

Repeat 5–8 times.

- Extend evenly through your spine, allowing sternum to lift and shoulder blades to release down.
- Press gently into the roller, allowing the roller assist you into spinal extension, lifting upper body.
- Experience more space between each segment of your spine as you lengthen your spine to the floor.

Mermaid

Benefits

Mobilizes spine during side bending; integrates core and upper body.

Starting Position

Sit tall with aligned spine, legs crossed. Place one hand on the roller alongside you.

Movement Sequence

Inhale

Lengthen through your spine and lift free arm up overhead.

Exhale

Activate core and bend sideways from top of spine to bottom, rolling the roller out to side.

Inhale

Slowly lengthen your spine to vertical from the bottom to top, as you roll the roller toward you. Arm again reaches overhead.

Exhale

Lower your arm alongside your body.

Repeat 3–5 times on each side.

- Allow your head and neck follow to the line of the rest of your spine; shoulder blades glide smoothly.
- Press gently into the roller, experiencing your strong center supporting your body during movement.
- Feel both sit bones sinking into the floor, as your pelvis counterbalances your spine movements.
- Alternate starting position: Sit on a cushion, or with legs long.

Diagonal Mermaid

Benefits
Mobilizes spine; integrates core and upper body.

Starting Position
Sit tall with legs crossed. Place the roller diagonally in front of one knee, and rotate your torso around your central axis, resting both hands on the roller.

Movement Sequence
To prepare—inhale; breath expands three-dimensionally.

Exhale
Activate core, gently curving your spine as you roll the roller diagonally away from your body.

Inhale
Slowly lengthen your spine to vertical from the bottom to top, maintaining rotation, as you roll the roller toward you.

Repeat 3–5 times on each side.

- First rotate your spine around your central axis, then flex forward as your arms press the roller away.
- Press gently into the roller, experiencing your strong center supporting your body during movement.
- As you roll the roller away from your body, curve your spine as far as feels comfortable.
- Feel both sit bones sinking into the floor, as your pelvis counterbalances your spine movements.

Lunge Series

Benefits

Integrates whole body movement.

Starting Position

From kneeling position, place one foot on the floor as far forward as feels comfortable. Legs hip-width apart, shoulders relaxed, hands gently holding ends of roller.

Movement Sequence

Inhale

Lift your arms and roller overhead, allowing gliding motion of shoulder blades.

Exhale

Activate core muscles, and allow your pelvis to move slowly forward, lengthening the front of your hip and thigh of the leg on the floor.

Inhale

Maintain lunge position.

Exhale

With strong core, allow your pelvis to move forward even further.

- Experience your strong center supporting your body throughout movement.
- During lunge, be certain your front foot is forward enough to allow your pelvis to move forward.
- Feel muscle filaments at the front of your hip and thigh sliding apart as your pelvis moves forward.
- Keep the roller centered above your head throughout exercise, with shoulders, neck, and jaw relaxed.
- Allow your pelvis to stay centered throughout lunge series, moving as far as feels comfortable.

Add rotation:

Maintain lunge position, arms lifted overhead holding roller.

Movement Sequence

To prepare—inhale; breath expands.

Exhale

Slowly rotate your upper body and arms in one direction.

Inhale

Return to centered lunge position.

Exhale

Slowly rotate upper body and arms in other direction.

Inhale

Return to centered lunge position.

Add side bending:

Maintain lunge position, arms lifted overhead holding roller.

Movement Sequence

To prepare—inhale; breath expands.

Exhale

Slowly bend your torso toward one side, arms gently pressing into roller.

Inhale

Return to centered lunge position.

Exhale

Slowly bend your torso to opposite side.

Inhale

Return to centered lunge position.

Exhale

Activate core, and slowly move your pelvis and your arms back to the starting position.

Repeat series 1–2 times each side.

PRO-ROLLER™ Pilates Essentials

Breathing
page 8

Imprint and Release
page 9

Ribcage Arms
page 10

Spine Rolls
page 11

Knee Lift
page 12

Bend and Stretch
page 13

Shoulder Reach
page 14

Shoulder Blade Squeeze
page 15

Arm Scissors
page 16

V to W
page 17

Arm Circles
page 18

Arm Wrap
page 19

Abdominal Curl
page 20

Dying Bug
page 21

Breast Stroke
page 22

Shell Stretch
page 23

Hundred
page 24

Mid-Back Extension
page 25

Half Roll Back
page 26

Obliques Roll Back
page 27

At a glance, these small photos reference each *PRO-ROLLER*™ *Pilates Essentials* exercise.

Spine Twist
page 28

Cat Stretch
page 29

Leg Extension
page 30

Knee Stretch
page 31

Saw
page 32

Triceps Press
page 33

Bridge
page 34

Hip Release
page 35

Toe Taps
page 36

Bookends
page 37

Leg Scissors
page 38

Bicycle
page 39

Frog Legs
page 40

Hip Sway
page 41

One Leg Kick
page 42

Sternum Drop
page 43

Spine Stretch Forward
page 44

Swan
page 45

Mermaid
page 46

Lunge Series
page 48

Today, I will...

PRO-ROLLER™ Pilates Essentials invites you to playfully experience movement that directly teaches your body and mind, with exercises that are fun and enjoyable. Adding the PRO-ROLLER™ helps you relax your tight, tense muscles and activate your less-toned muscles for balanced tone and body symmetry. The PRO-ROLLER™ effectively integrates Pilates movements into a whole body experience, connecting you with your body for greater understanding, and integrating mind and body to create a life of balance, purpose, and joy. Are you ready to get rolling toward a happy, healthy body?

Acknowledgements

Special thanks to my sons Quinn and Zane Sullivan for their continual inspiration, love, and laughter.

References

Franklin, Eric, *Beautiful Body, Beautiful Mind: The Power of Positive Imagery,* (NJ: Princeton Book Company, 2009).

Franklin, Eric, *Dynamic Alignment Through Imagery,* (IL: Human Kinetics, 1996).

Franklin, Eric, *Inner Focus, Outer Strength: Using Imagery and Exercise for Health, Strength and Beauty,* (NJ: Princeton Book Company, 2006).

Pilates, Joseph, *Return to Life Through Contrology,* (NY: J.J. Augustine, 1945).

Learn more

OPTP
www.optp.com

Franklin Method
www.franklinmethod.com

Pilates Method Alliance
www.pilatesmethodalliance.org

Stott Pilates
www.stottpilates.com

About the author

Angela Kneale, OTR, is an occupational therapist, certified Stott Pilates instructor, and Franklin Method educator. She is the author of *Desk Pilates, Sanctband® Pilates Essentials, Pro-Roller® Massage Essentials,* and *Stretch Out® Strap Pilates Essentials*. Angela has incorporated Pilates into her therapy practice for more than fifteen years. She enjoys teaching, and specializes in the integration of movement, breathing, postural alignment, and relaxation techniques for optimal health, with particular interest in individual, corporate, and community wellness. www.EmbodyHealthWellnessLIfe.com